YOUR THERAPIST FRIEND

NAVVEE B

This book is for all the teenagers who go crazy every third day ;)

<u>*Actually I'm 16 too which means I go crazy every third day too,hmm kinda enough for us to have a man to man conversation without having the fear of being judged...*</u>

Contents

Preface   *vii*

1. The Very Foremost Thing Important For You Is To "be Kind To Yourself"   1

2. Whatever You're Going Through,you Will Soon Get Through. Remind Yourself This Each Time You Feel Low And Watch How You Overcome These "lows"   2

3. A Pause Because I'm Currently Feeling Like Shit   4

4. Dance When You're Sad,don't Cry.trust Me On This.   5

5. Just Know   6

6. Feelings Are Simply Feelings,nothing Else.   7

7. Liking Someone Is Okay,loving Someone To Me Is Not.   8

8. Listen-it's Okay If You Don't Have It Figured Out Right Now.   10

9. Torn Between Wanting Them And Wanting To Get Over Them   11

10. The "i Don't Know What's Wrong" Phase.   12

11. Thought Filtering   13

12. Things You Probably Wish Someone Would Tell You.   14

Remind Yourself All These Things And Fall For Yourself And God Truly And Deeply.   17

Preface

Mental health.AHHH M-E-N-T-A-L F-R-E-A-K-I-N-G H-E-A-L-T-H

Well,let's normalise it first.

Mental health refers to the psychological & emotional well being of a human.

it is so important to have a stable mental state,like sooooooo important.

I have no idea how to write a book so honestly im just telling my advices and POVs to you guys and also My friends call me "the therapist friend" so I find no reason to not help y'all.

1

The very foremost thing important for YOU is to "be kind to yourself"

———♡———

Life.The concept of life is very complex.It's unfair,Sometimes We feel like we absolutely love it and sometimes things get so bad that we start to feel like "What's even the point of me being alive bro?" "nobody loves me" "i will never ever be happy again" and what not.

KNOWING that you will eventually be alright,things will settle and you won't feel the same anymore,Eventually.

but you know what I think is IF ONLY we knew that being hard on ourselves and overthinking literally does us NO good???hmm??think about it..

You are all you have and will EVER have.Don't let anyone tell you things othwerwise.You were born alone,all by yourself(and also your mum) and you will leave and die all alone.(sadly without your mum).You have to learn to be okay by yourself and come onnnnn i know you Can. and even you know.

Stop feeling pity for yourself and start loving yourself.Yes,This is the sign.

Atleast you can just not talk bad about yourself to ANYONE OR EVEN YOURSELF baby.trust me you can.

2

Whatever you're going through, You will soon get through. Remind yourself this each time you feel low and watch how you overcome these "lows"

to believe that things will get better someday is STRENGTH in itself.

to believe sun will rise again and one day,that sunrise won't make your heart feel as heavy as you thought it would.

it takes courage to prove the denial inside you wrong which tells you that "nothing will ever change,you'll drown".

If you can simply tell yourself that THINGS WILL BE FINE ONE DAY,then trust me YOU CAN PULL YOURSELF OUT OF ANYTHING.yes ANYTHING.

Have faith in God,He sent you here for a purpose.You have a purpose.You are precious.

precious to God,to your parents.to any stranger you're about to make feel good.You really are my lil munchkin ;)

3

a pause because i'm currently feeling like shit

———♡———

hah anyways I'll get over it.

4

Dance when you're sad, don't cry. Trust me on this.

———♡———

So it's like obvious--cry when you know you need to,but when you feel that you're not liking this crying thing right now but you're still crying ,Just Get up and DANCEEEEEE

IT WILL MAKE U FEEL SUPERGOOD I ASSURE.I dont care if you dont know how to dance,just get up and dance.Dance like it's your last day on this planet.Dance like you're drunk(every teenager knows how to act drunk while not being actually drunk)Sweat the shit out.It's honestly so much better than wasting your tears over someone or some bad thoughts(they are no worse than a really really bad person,you know.)which won't probably even matter in an year or two

Turn the music on or put your earphones on and Dance.even if its for 10 minutes.It will help.You'll know when you'll feel the change.You will,and for sure.

5

Just know

When things are not going your way,they're going his way and do you think what He has planned for you can do you anywrong?

Well,if you ask me then I honestly don't think so and if u don't wanna ask me then too it's fine.

Firstly,I'm talking about God.not your ex boyfriend or school crush...okay.

God has plans.It is all about faith;trust & patience.

real faith is when you're ready to accept whatever comes your way as-the will of God.

God has made you so gently and carefully.You are so strong and bful.you just need to keep reminding yourself this or otherwise i'll get mad at you.I'm very short tempered at times.I really will. hahaha

If I,being a 16 year old can trust God this much,then you can as well.

6

Feelings are simply feelings, nothing else.

Saying this is as easy as-you telling yourself that I'm gonna get this in my head,is.

feelings omygod they're so gross to me and to you too..maybe?or probably. (all thanks to our wonderful experiences)

this feeling to have feelings sounds good only in the matter of temporary happiness.yes.I know you agree.

Sadness-anger-love-calmness-relief-numbness-*having butterflies is a newly discovered feeling too*

they are simply feelings that stay very inconstant almost each time.they pass.they do not stay if you don't let them.It's all in your control.

so why would you even stress for a second, about something so inconsistent and WHOLLY temporary in your world?

i would never.

7

Liking someone is okay, Loving someone to me is not.

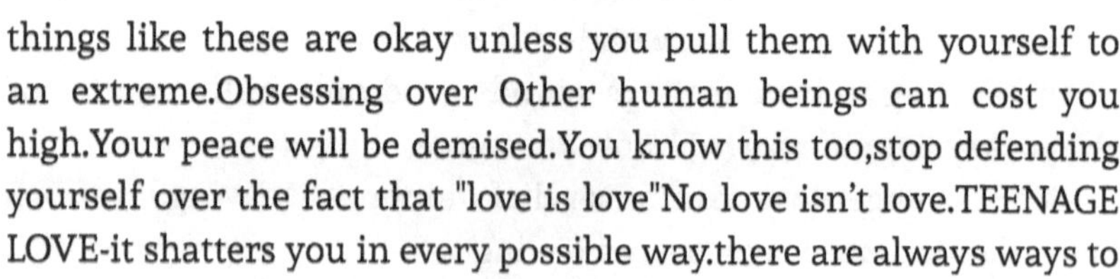

things like these are okay unless you pull them with yourself to an extreme.Obsessing over Other human beings can cost you high.Your peace will be demised.You know this too,stop defending yourself over the fact that "love is love"No love isn't love.TEENAGE LOVE-it shatters you in every possible way.there are always ways to escape.

Don't let anyone have that power when they start to dictate to your daily moods-happiness or sadness.

Love is what you think you have for your VERY OWN SELF,FAMILY,FRIENDS,and GOD.

Do not let anyone fool you please.Don't settle especially in your teenage or early 20s(bcs you're not in your senses and know really lesser than needed during this period)

"I love you"is just a phase and literally,anyone can fake being into you these days.(this generation is cursed,completely.)

Love costs nothing if it's between you and you,if its between you and someone you know who is right to love.

SPOIL YOUR OWN SELF,LOVE YOUR OWN SELF AND NEVER UNDERESTIMATE THE POWER OF SELF LOVE AND GOD'S LOVE.this is it.

9

8

Listen-It's okay if you don't have it figured out right now.

family-issues,carrier-stress,school,friendships,situationships and what not.

Bro why have you put so much burden on yourself?you have your whole life to figure it out,Don't you?and also just don't think i'm telling you to do nothing.I'm telling you that You DO have alot of time to figure it out.Whatever you're thinking about 24*7,Yes that.Things will fall into place.They get scattered so that they can be on their places.Don't put so much pressure on yourself.you're just a soft small baby right now.

"My little munchkin.You're too cute to be stressing this much."Comfort yourself by whispering this when you find yourself thinking too much about any or everything.

9

Torn between wanting them and wanting to get over them

listen-nobody on this whole planet is worth losing yourself to.yes.nobody.

If they left you,so what?their loss,isn't it?yes it is.

Why would you want to be with someone who can risk losing such a pretty soul like you?

they left bcs they weren't meant to be there in the first place.it's not your fault okay?

you know you did it all.whatever that could be done to make them stay.If they don't see it,consider them blind and move on .

if they don't see your worth,don't help them to see it anyway.they're simply and clearly blind.**pray for them**.and start to love yourself in the corners you THOUGHT they loved you.you won't regret.

you are an independent person.you don't need them,you never did.you had a life before them,you'll have one after them.

10

The "I don't know what's wrong" phase.

————♡————

firstly,know that this too shall pass.It's a phase.A phase can do nothing to sucha strongass person like you(yes,you).

I know it's a terrible feeling.You may know nothing's even wrong but still feel this way.

It's a feeling.a tiny little miserable feeling.If you don't let it be all over you,it won't be.No matter what.And I'm serious.

Know that having to feel different feelings is a privilige,Thank God for it.And feel it all.

I once read a quote on pinterest that said "cry as much as you want to,but when you stop

make sure that you never cry over the same reason again."

look if you're sad over some person,just know that getting sad over <u>any</u> person for more than a week is as silly as that person(probably).

and if you're sad over some like reallyyyy serious reason,know that it will pass :) God has your back,He is preparing for better things.okay?

11
Thought Filtering

Filtering your thoughts is a complete game changer.

what you tell your mind and yourself is the way how you choose to communicate with your soul.

Please don't be mean and loud to yourself.you don't deserve that.

You're so kind to others and so harsh to yourself.This is unfair.

Make sure you stay soft .

Make sure you are your own before you are someone else's.

12

Things You probably wish someone would tell you.

———❤———

-Sometimes people are going to learn you just to hurt you and that's completely okay,you're gonna be perfectly fine.Eventually.

-You must be aware of the fact that you're good and beautiful as hell.If someone doesn't see it then something's probably wrong with their eyes.Not your bad.Okay?

-Forgive your past self and try to heal.She's the old you and deserves to be loved and forgiven too.

-There's nothing that stressing out,hating and anger can give you and-love,kindness and patience cannot.

-Life's too short for doing anything that doesn't feel right.Yes-trust me on this.

-They're no longer in your life because God chose not to put them in your fate.Trust what he does.

-There's nothing wrong with being vulnerable.It means you're a healthy human.

-You don't have to be scared to walk alone.You're literally the bestest friend you can ever have.FOR LIFE.

-Keep your friends close and God closer.

-You seriously don't need to have a lover during your teenage to make you feel happy.You can literally get sooooo happy just by yourself and one or two good friends.Trust me on this my cutie.

-Don't ever beat yourself up regarding literally anything.Not a single thing is worthy of making yourself feel like shit.

-Unfortunately life is going to be unfair.It's not going to be easy at times.but you know what can be easy?How softly and lovingly you handle yourself and things you care about.

-Real love isn't going to hurt you.It's not going to make you feel heavy.Don't let stupid Instagram posts fool you.

-Never bear disrespect.I repeat never.You're worthy of endless respect and love sp make sure you stand by telling yourself this everytime you know you need to.

-You don't always have to project things.People treat you the way they feel about you.Don't delay your blessings by analyzing their follies.

-Have boundaries and know that its a privilege for others to get to know you.But alongside,stay humble,fear God,do right.

-Do what you want to do.Utilise your time in that course.the time is going to go anyway.

-Write how you feel instead of constantly thinking about it.

-If only you knew that overthinking literally does no good.

-Do what you have to do until you can do what you want to do.

-Do what's right not what's easy.

-Temporary pleasure will get you in troube.It's a sure thing.So you better learn how to say a No.

-Silence the voice in your head that says it won't ever get better,that you're not worthy of reciprocated love.You really can have control all over this and when you do trust me-things will begin to change.

-Don't hate on people who do you wrong.Just Pray for them and forgive them.

-You don't have to be the type to hurt people.you cannot afford that Karma.Noone can.

-Everything happening to you is the result of your past karmas.You cannot do anything about it and have faith but YOU can make sure you never repeat those same mistakes again.

-Think before you speak.

-The world doesn't need anymore nonchalance so if you think you're the one who cares,please stay the same.I appreciate you.The world needs you.You are God's favorite,and probably mine too.

-You're not going through that because you're bad or you deserve it.You're going through that because you're still unknown of the fact that you're strong enough to go through such hard days.Keep going.

-No you're not a burden.No you're not a mistake.

-It's okay to seek for help.It doesn't make you any less of an independent and strong person.

-You're amazing and yet have so many cute little(or maybe quite hard but worthy)journeys to go through.

-You're going to be proud of yourself in an year and feel so funny thinking about how you thought you're life seemed pointlesss.

-Remember to love you and spread love around you.

-Love is such a pretty word and so are you.

I love you.

Remind Yourself All These Things And Fall For
Yourself And God Truly And Deeply.

Treat yourself the way you'd treat someone you loved.
Fall in love with doing things that make you feel alive.Literally.
I'd so much more to say but I think I should now just shut up.